Real-time Japan in Basic English

Asahi Press

音声再生アプリ「リスニング・トレーナー」を使った 音声ダウンロード

朝日出版社開発のアプリ、「リスニング・トレーナー（リストレ）」を使えば、教科書の音声を
スマホ、タブレットに簡単にダウンロードできます。どうぞご活用ください。

◉ アプリ【リスニング・トレーナー】の使い方

《アプリのダウンロード》

App Store または Google Play から
「リスニング・トレーナー」のアプリ
（無料）をダウンロード

App Storeは
こちら▶

Google Playは
こちら▶

《アプリの使い方》

① アプリを開き「コンテンツを追加」をタップ
② 画面上部に【15671】を入力しDoneをタップ

音声ストリーミング配信 》》》

この教科書の音声は、
右記ウェブサイトにて
無料で配信しています。 https://text.asahipress.com/free/english/

表紙デザイン：葛籠貫 智宏

Real-time Japan in Basic English
Copyright © 2021 by Asahi Press

まえがき

　現在、グローバル化の流れの中でTOEICやTOEFLなどを活用して英語力の向上を図るとともに、とりわけ話す・書くなどの発信型の英語運用能力の育成が強く求められています。教材研究会ではこの数年間にわたり、基礎英文法の習熟度とその活用を課題にしてアンケート等の実態調査を行ってきました。その結果、多くの学生が自分の英語力のなさに苦しみながらも使える英語力の習得に強い意欲を持っていることが明らかになりました。

　当研究会は教材を編集するにあたって、基礎英文法の習熟度と活用力、日本文化の発信、学習の仕方の提案、といった3点を課題にしました。英文法については中学・高校でほぼすべての項目を学習したことになっています。学校で学んだ英文法を確実に修得していれば、日常生活における基礎的なコミュニケーションは十分可能なはずです。しかし、多くの学生は英文法に対して負のイメージを持っており、英文法を活用する実践的な経験は十分ではありません。そのために結果としてコミュニケーションに必要な英語力が身についていないのが現状です。日本文化についての課題も明らかです。最近は多くの学生が海外研修や留学を経験するようになりました。そうした学生が語るのは、語彙力や文法力のなさだけでなく、日本の文化に対する知識不足です。日常の身近な文化を英語で伝える経験をもっと積む必要があるようです。最後は学び方の問題です。アンケートの結果では、一人で英語を学ぶより皆で学ぶことを好む学生が多くなってきています。ペアやグループで学習を行う協働学習の手法は言い換えればアクティブ・ラーニングです。英語を学ぶ動機の一つはコミュニケーション能力の獲得です。アクティブ・ラーニングの手法を取り入れることで、仲間とのかかわりが生まれ、授業が楽しい場になると思われます。

　本教材の活用をとおして、一人でも多くの学生が英語で発信する自信を身につけることができれば幸いです。

大学英語教育学会（JACET）教材研究会

Jenks, Daniel（千葉大学）

見上　晃（拓殖大学）

大山 中勝（千葉大学名誉教授）

鈴木 彩子（玉川大学）

高橋 貞雄（玉川大学名誉教授）

構 成

☐ **Vocabulary**
　各章のトピックに関連する語彙の確認。以後の活動への取り組みを促します。

☐ **Listen and fill in the blanks**
　各章の文法項目に焦点を当てた和文英訳リスニング。汎用性の高い例文に習熟します。

☐ **Listen, complete the dialogue and interact**
　英問英答式のリスニング。日本文化について尋ねられた時に応答する練習。主にペア活動として活用します。音源を使わない場合には自分で英文を考えて応じる練習も可能です。

☐ **Grammar**
　各章で焦点を当てている文法の解説と確認。練習問題をとおして用例の使われ方を学びます。

☐ **Before you read**
　Read and Think につなぐ活動。各章のトピックに関連させて自分の考えをまとめ、友達と意見交換を行います。

☐ **Read and Think**
(1) 本文の内容理解を確認するためのTFクイズ、または英問英答。
(2) Grammar hunting
　　各章で取り上げた文法項目を本文の中で確認する活動。
(3) What do you think?
　　本文の中で扱われている内容に関連させて、それぞれの考えを述べる活動。

☐ **Active Plus**
　アクティブ・ラーニングを想定した発展的な活動。個人で取り組むことも可能ですが、できるだけペアやグループで行いましょう。

☐ **Reflection**
　学習の振り返り。各章のトピックと文法について、十分に習得することができた(5)、全くできなかった(1)のように点数をつけて自己評価を行います。

☐ **World Quiz**
　各章のトピックに関連したクイズ。

目次

Real-time Japan in Basic English

Asahi Press

Starter Reflection & Goal Setting
日本のことを英語で伝えるために

アンケートに答え、自分が日本のことを英語で伝えられるようになるための課題をみつけよう。

課題 1 以下のABCのそれぞれの項目について、当てはまると思う数字を書き入れてみよう。

1. そう思う	2. やや思う	3. 判断できない	4. あまり思わない	5. そう思わない

[A] 自分がどう思うかを書いてみよう。

1. （　）日本人の英語力の一つとして、日本文化を伝える力が必要である。
2. （　）自分は外国でまたは外国籍の人に日本文化を英語で伝える自信がある。
3. （　）英語の授業でもっと日本文化を伝える練習が必要である。
4. （　）日本文化を英語で伝えることが難しい原因は文法力の弱さである。
5. （　）日本文化を英語で伝えることが難しい原因は単語力の弱さである。
6. （　）日本文化を英語で伝えることが難しい原因は日本文化をよく知らないことである。

[B] 一般的な印象を書いてみよう。

1. （　）歌舞伎などの伝統文化を伝える英語力が必要である。
2. （　）遊びや趣味などの身の回りのことを伝える英語力が必要である。
3. （　）日本の衣食住について伝える英語力が必要である。
4. （　）祝日などの日本の行事について伝える英語力が必要である。
5. （　）学校などの日本の教育制度について伝える英語力が必要である。
6. （　）日本の政治や経済について伝える英語力が必要である。
7. （　）日本の地理や風土について伝える英語力が必要である。
8. （　）日本の歴史について伝える英語力が必要である。

[C] 自分のことを書いてみよう。

1. （　）自分は祝日などの日本の行事について英語で伝えることができる。
2. （　）自分は日本の政治や経済について英語で伝えることができる。
3. （　）自分は遊びや趣味などの身の回りのことを英語で伝えることができる。
4. （　）自分は学校などの日本の教育制度について英語で伝えることができる。
5. （　）自分は日本の歴史について英語で伝えることができる。
6. （　）自分は日本の地理や風土について英語で伝えることができる。
7. （　）自分は歌舞伎などの伝統文化を英語で伝えることができる。
8. （　）自分は日本の衣食住について英語で伝えることができる。

Chapter 1

課題2 外国で、または外国籍の人に日本のことについて伝えたいことをその順に書いてみよう（3つでなくてもよい）。

1. _____
2. _____
3. _____

課題3 日本のことについて何を英語で伝えるのが難しいか、その順に書いてみよう（3つでなくてもよい）。

1. _____
2. _____
3. _____

《振り返り1》
アンケートをとおして、自分にとって最も課題だと思うことを書き出してみよう。

《振り返り2》
グループで情報交換し、共通する課題を見つけて書き出してみよう。

《学習目標の設定》
この授業をとおして、自分が最も学びたいこと、身につけたいことを書いてみよう。

TOPIC **Greetings and Manners**
日本式挨拶とマナー

GRAMMAR 動詞の種類：文型

Vocabulary

単語の確認をしよう。(**I know** ☑, **I don't know** ?)

1. ☐ hug (　) 　　2. ☐ handshaking (　) 　　3. ☐ bow (　) 　　4. ☐ senior (　)
5. ☐ encounter (　) 　6. ☐ respect (　) 　　7. ☐ consideration (　)
8. ☐ humbleness (　) 　9. ☐ customer (　) 　10. ☐ invite (　)

a. おじぎ	b. 握手	c. 招く	d. 出会う	e. 思いやり
f. 謙虚	g. 年長者	h. 客	i. 敬意	j. 抱擁する

🎧 |2| **Listen and fill in the blanks.**

1. 握手は仕事の挨拶で一般的な方法です。
   (　　　　　　) is a popular form of business (　　　　　).

2. 目上の人にファースト・ネームで呼びかけてはいけません。
   You should not (　　　　　) your (　　　　　) by their first names.

3. 名刺は一種の身分証明書です。
   Meishi or business cards are a (　　　　　) of (　　　　　) card.

4. エスカレーターでは片側に並びます。
   People (　　　　　) up on one side on the (　　　　　).

5. 喫煙はほとんどすべての公共施設で禁止されています。
   Smoking is (　　　　　) in almost all (　　　　　) facilities.

6. 微笑むと会話がスムーズに運びます。
   Smiles (　　　　　) conversation (　　　　　) smoothly.

7. バスや電車の中では電話で話してはいけません。
   You must not talk (　　　　　) the (　　　　　) on the bus or the train.

8. お風呂の中ではシャンプーや石鹸は禁止です。
   Don't use (　　　　　) or soap in the (　　　　　).

🎧 |3| **Listen, complete the dialogue and interact.**

1. A: Do I have to give the taxi driver a tip?
   B: _____

2. A: I heard someone say "*domo*" as a greeting. What does it mean?
   B: _____

3. A: Do you say anything before or after the meal?
   B: _____

4. A: What does "priority seat" mean?
   B: _____

GRAMMAR 動詞の種類：文型

動詞によって文の構造（文型）が決まります。英語の文のほとんどが以下のような５つの文型に分類されます。英文を作るときには特に動詞の働きに留意するようにしよう。

(S(ubject) = 主語、V(erb) = 動詞、C(omplement) = 補語、O(bject) = 目的語)

第１文型：S + V
第２文型：S + V + C
第３文型：S + V + O
第４文型：S + V + O + O
第５文型：S + V + O + C

[I] 以下のa～eの英文が日本語の意味に合うように（　）に適当な動詞を入れ、それぞれがどの文型になるかを説明しよう。

a. Many people (　　　　　　　) kind.（第＿＿文型）
   多くの人は親切です。

b. I (　　　　　　　) my mother a thank-you letter.（第＿＿文型）
   私は母に感謝の手紙を送りました。

c. Japanese people often (　　　　　　　).（第＿＿文型）
   日本人は微笑むことが多いです。

d. The present (　　　　　　　) her happy.（第＿＿文型）
   プレゼントは彼女を嬉しい気持ちにさせました。

e. You must not (　　　　　　　) away your litter on the street.（第＿＿文型）
   通りにゴミを捨ててはいけません。

[II] 以下の英文の（　）の語句のどちらかを選んで正しい英文を作り、それぞれの意味を言ってみよう。

a. May I introduce (me, myself)?

b. Will you (tell, teach) me your name?

c. The Japanese culture book (looks, looks at) interesting.

d. I had my purse (steal, stolen).

e. My friend Ken invited me (his birthday party, to his birthday party).

[III] 以下の英文を指示に従って書き換えよう。

a. I gave a nod of greeting to my boss.（第４文型に）

_____

b. The audience gave the artist a big hand.（受動態の文に）

_____

Before you read

以下の項目を読み、どう思うか数字を書き入れてみよう。

| 1. そう思う | 2. 少しそう思う | 3. あまりそう思わない | 4. そう思わない |

1. (　) Japanese people often hug each other.
2. (　) When visiting someone's house, Japanese people usually bring a small gift.
3. (　) Young people give their seats to elderly people.
4. (　) When people talk, they look each other in the eye.

次にグループをつくり、みんなの考えを表にしてみよう。

友人の名前	1問	2問	3問	4問

🎧 |4| Read and Think

The foundations of Japanese manners are consideration and hospitality. Since Japan is an island country, people must live together and help each other. Partly for this reason, humbleness is considered important, and boasting is not appreciated. One example of this is seen when giving a present. Japanese people often say *tsumaranai mono desu ga* (literally "It's a trivial thing"), even when they hope the present will be liked. People think hospitality or *omotenashi* valuable in business situations as well as daily life. The main belief is that customers always come first.

If you are ever invited inside someone's house as a guest, there is one very important point to remember. You must take off your shoes at the entrance.

(1) Answer the questions.

1. What are bases of manners in Japan?

_____

2. Why is humbleness appreciated in Japan?

_____

3. What is the essence of *omotenashi*?

_____

4. What is important when you enter someone's house?

_____

(2) Grammar hunting.

第５文型（SVOC）の文がどこにあるか探してみよう。

(3) What do you think?

"*tsumaranai mono desu ga*" という言い方をどのように思いますか？また、なぜそう思いますか？

Active Plus

◇以下の英文は日本人のどのようなしぐさや行動について述べているのでしょうか？

1. When Japanese people beckon a person, it is done with the hand palm down with a raking motion.

2. Many Japanese people don't like to stare at each other's eyes while they're talking.

3. When Japanese people are offered a second helping, they usually don't accept straight away.

◇上記のそれぞれのしぐさや行動で誤解を招く可能性があるとしたらどのようなことでしょうか？ みんなで意見を出し合ってみよう。

_____

_____

◇レストランで蕎麦を食べている時に外国の方に肩をすぼめられたことがありました。お蕎麦を食べる時にはズルズルと音を立てながら食べても大丈夫だということを伝える英文を考えて言ってみよう。

_____

_____

Reflection

この課で学んだことを評価しよう。

トピックの Can-do		1	2	3	4	5				
文法の Can-do	理解 1 2 3 4 5						活用 1 2 3 4 5			
コメント										

こぶしとこぶしを合わせる挨拶のルーツはどこの国？

1. Italy　　2. New Zealand　　3. Jamaica

3 Chapter

TOPIC **Seasonal Events in Japan**
日本の季節と行事

GRAMMAR 文の種類

Vocabulary

単語の確認をしよう。(**I know** ☑ , **I don't know** ?)

1. □ divide (   ) 2. □ variety (   ) 3. □ traditionally (   ) 4. □ arrival (   )
5. □ throw (   ) 6. □ drive away (   ) 7. □ celebrate (   )
8. □ hang (   ) 9. □ seasonal (   ) 10. □ modern (   )

a. 現代の	b. つるす	c. 追い払う	d. 伝統的に	e. 季節の
f. 祝う	g. 投げる	h. 多様さ	i. 分ける	j. 到着

🎧 5 Listen and fill in the blanks.

1. 日本では新年度は4月から始まり、子供たちは進級します。

   In Japan, the new school year starts (   ) April (   ) children move to the next grade.

2. 多くの日本人は最新のテクノロジーを楽しむ一方で、節分のような古い伝統も大切にしています。

   (   ) many Japanese people enjoy advanced technology, they (   ) old traditions, such as *setsubun*.

3. 日本人は「花」と言ったら、桜を思い浮かべます。

   (   ) Japanese people say "blossom," they think (   ) cherry blossoms.

4. 成人の日に20歳の若者は成人になったことを祝福されます。

   On Coming of Age Day, young people (   ) twenty are (   ) on their maturity.

5. 5月5日はこどもの日で私たちは子供たちの成長と幸福をお祝いします。

   May 5th is Children's Day (   ) we celebrate children's growth (   ) happiness.

6. 9月は暦の上では秋ですが、まだまだ暑い日が多いです。

   (   ) September is in fall (   ) to the calendar, we still have many hot days.

🎧 6 Listen, complete the dialogue and interact.

1. A: What is Japanese summer like?
   B: _____

2. A: Do you usually have snow in winter in Tokyo?
   B: _____

3. A: Why don't you like spring? It's a beautiful season!
   B: _____

4. A: Which season would be the best to come to Japan for foreign travelers?
   B: _____

❀ 8

GRAMMAR 文の種類

文は構造と内容の両面から分類することができます。文を構造から分類すると、主として次の3通りに分けることができます。1) 単文（Simple Sentence）：S＋Vが1つの文、2) 重文（Compound Sentence）：S＋Vが2つ以上あり、それぞれが等位接続詞（and, but, orなど）で結ばれている文、3) 複文（Complex Sentence）：S＋Vが2つ以上あり、それぞれが従位接続詞（that, when, ifなど）や関係詞（who, whichなど）で導かれる文。時には重文や複文が入り混じった複雑な文が見られることもあります。また、文の内容面という点からは、1) 平叙文（Declarative Sentence）、2) 疑問文（Interrogative Sentence）、3) 命令文（Imperative Sentence）、4) 感嘆文（Exclamatory Sentence）に分類できます。

[Ⅰ] 以下のa~dの英文が日本語の意味に合うように（　　　）に適当な語を入れ、それぞれ単文、重文、複文のどれかを説明してみよう。

a. February 3rd is *setsubun*, which is also (　　　　　　　) Bean Throwing Day.
2月3日は節分で、豆まきの日とも言われます。　　　　　　　　　　　　（＿＿＿＿文）

b. The third Monday of September is a day to (　　　　　) respect to the aged.
敬老の日は老人に敬意を示す日です。　　　　　　　　　　　　　　　　（＿＿＿＿文）

c. Many people eat soba (　　　　　　) they celebrate *shogatsu* or New Year.
多くの人は正月を迎える前にお蕎麦を食べます。　　　　　　　　　　　（＿＿＿＿文）

d. For the duration of the Obon Festival many businesses are closed (　　　　　) many people return to their hometowns.　　　　　　　　　　　　（＿＿＿＿文）
お盆の期間には多くの企業が休業し、里帰りする人がたくさんいます。

[Ⅱ] 以下の英文の（　　　）の語句のどちらかを選んで正しい英文を作り、それぞれの意味を言ってみよう。

a. Before (went , going) to bed, I said *oyasuminasai* to my family.

b. On Children's Day my parents planted a cherry tree (wish, wishing) for my health and happiness.

c. On the evening of Halloween children go around their neighbors saying "Trick (and, or) treat!".

d. Why do people (wash, washing) their hands before they pray at a shrine or a temple?

[Ⅲ] 以下の英文はどのような文構造になっているか分析してみよう。

In the legend of the Star Festival, it is said that a couple of stars who loved each other very much stopped working, so the angry Emperor separated them, but allowed them to meet once a year.

Before you read

四季の中で一番好きな季節は何ですか。また好きではない季節は何ですか。その理由を簡単に書いてみよう。

The season I like best: _____

Reason: _____

The season I don't like: _____

Reason: _____

次にグループをつくり、みんなの考えを表にしてみよう。

友人の名前	好きな季節	理由	好きではない季節	理由

Read and Think

|7|

In Japan, a year is divided into four seasons and a new year starts from spring. Each season has special events and holidays. For example, February 3rd is *setsubun*. Traditionally people think that this is the beginning of spring. On this day, people throw soybeans around their houses to drive away evil spirits. It is believed that doing so can help them live healthily and happily for the coming year.

Another example is *tanabata* on July 7th. This is also known as the Star Festival, and people celebrate the arrival of summer on this day. When *tanabata* comes, they write their wishes on strips of paper and hang them on bamboo trees.

Japanese people enjoy the changing of the seasons. These seasonal events show the Japanese love of nature. Although the country is famous for its modern technology, people still live with nature and enjoy its variety.

(1) Answer the questions.

1. When does the new year start in Japan?

_____

2. Why do people throw soybeans on *setsubun*?

_____

3. What do people do on *tanabata*?

_____

4. What do the seasonal events show?

_____

(2) Grammar hunting.

英文から単文、重文、複文を一つずつ書き出してみよう。次にそれぞれの文の主語・動詞を丸で囲みましょう。

単文：＿＿＿＿＿＿＿＿＿＿＿＿＿＿＿＿＿＿＿＿＿＿＿＿＿＿＿＿＿＿＿＿＿＿＿

重文：＿＿＿＿＿＿＿＿＿＿＿＿＿＿＿＿＿＿＿＿＿＿＿＿＿＿＿＿＿＿＿＿＿＿＿

複文：＿＿＿＿＿＿＿＿＿＿＿＿＿＿＿＿＿＿＿＿＿＿＿＿＿＿＿＿＿＿＿＿＿＿＿

(3) What do you think?

地球温暖化が進み、日本でも夏は非常に暑い日、冬は暖かい日が増えてきました。地球温暖化を生じさせている原因は何だと思いますか。またその対策として、あなたは何ができるでしょうか。

Active Plus

◇以下の項目について、外国人に体験してもらいたいかどうか、あなたの考えを数字で書き入れてみよう。

1. ぜひ体験してもらいたい	2. できれば体験してもらいたい
3. 時間があれば体験してもらいたい	4. 体験してもらいたくない

1. (　　) Having a *hanami* party in spring

2. (　　) Going to a waterpark in summer

3. (　　) Doing *momiji-gari* in fall

4. (　　) Going to see Christmas lights in winter

◇あなたの友人はどう思うか尋ねてみよう。

友人の名前	1問	2問	3問	4問

◇あなたの考えと友人の考えを比べて異なる点やその理由などについて意見交換してみよう。

Reflection

この課で学んだことを評価しよう。

トピックのCan-do			1	2	3	4	5				
文法の Can-do	理解	1	2	3	4	5	活用	1	2	3	4	5
コメント											

World Quiz

旧正月には様々な催事があります。この水かけが行われるのは主にどこの国？

1. Spain　　2. Thailand　　3. Brazil

Chapter 4

TOPIC **Popular School Events**
人気のある学校行事

GRAMMAR 時制と相

Vocabulary

単語の確認をしよう。(**I know** ☑ , **I don't know** ?)

1. ☐ popular (　) 　　2. ☐ probably (　) 　　3. ☐ custom (　) 　　4. ☐ unique to (　)
5. ☐ excited (　) 　　6. ☐ compete (　) 　　7. ☐ neighbor (　) 　
8. ☐ cheer (　) 　　9. ☐ daylong (　) 　　10. ☐ different (　)

a. 競う	b. 違う	c. 人気のある	d. 近所の人	e. 終日の
f. おそらく	g. 興奮した	h. 風習	i. 特有な	j. 声援する

🎧 8 Listen and fill in the blanks.

1. 小学校で私が一番楽しみだった時間は給食です。
   The time I (　　　) forward to the most at elementary school (　　　) school lunch time.

2. 玉入れは日本の運動会に特有の競技です。
   "*Tama-ire*" (　　　) an activity exclusive (　　　) the *undokai*.

3. 玉入れでは、小さな子供たちがお手玉を棒の先に付けられた籠に入れることを競います。
   In the *tama-ire* game, young children (　　　) to throw beanbags into a basket (　　　) to the top of a pole.

4. 中学校で私が苦手だった教科は理科です。
   At junior high school the subject I (　　　) not good at (　　　) science.

5. 私たちのクラスは合唱コンクールで優勝しました。
   Our class (　　　) the top prize at our school (　　　) competition.

6. 私が高校で参加していた部活はバスケットボールです。
   The high school club activity I (　　　) in (　　　) basketball.

🎧 9 Listen, complete the dialogue and interact.

1. A: What is the bag Japanese elementary school pupils have?
   B: _____

2. A: What time did your school start in the morning?
   B: _____

3. A: Did your high school have a school uniform?
   B: _____

4. A: What do you think about school uniforms?
   B: _____

❀ 12

5. A: I don't know what the cultural festival is. What is it?

B: _____

GRAMMAR 時制と相

時（一般認識としての時間軸）は過去、現在、未来に分かれます。英語では、一般に、時は文法形式として時制（tense）と相（aspect）、それに副詞類を関連させて表します。英語の時制には過去と現在があります。助動詞のwillなどを未来形と呼ぶこともありますが、厳密に言えばwillは現在形です。その過去形はwouldです。相は動作や行為が継続しているか、完了しているかを表す文法形式です。前者は進行形（be+ing形）、後者は完了形（have+過去分詞形）で表します。時制と相を組み合わせて、さらにwillを使ってさまざまな文を作ることができます。

[Ⅰ] 以下のa～fは時制と相を組み合わせてできる文です。（　　）内に適当な語を入れて文を完成させよう。それぞれの語の最初の文字は指定されています。

a. Many schools in Japan (s　　　) in April.（単純現在形）

b. We are (p　　　) judo in the school gym.（現在進行形）

c. Paul and I have (k　　　) each other for five years.（現在完了形）

d. My friend (p　　　) EIKEN Grade 2 last month.（単純過去形）

e. We (w　　　) studying English when the earthquake struck.（過去進行形）

f. The train had already (l　　　) the station when I arrived.（過去完了形）

[Ⅱ] 以下の英文の（　　）の語句のどちらかを選んで正しい英文を作り、それぞれの意味を言ってみよう。

a. Our school dance team (will perform, has performed) in the afternoon tomorrow.（単純未来）

b. I (will study, will be studying) for entrance exams about this time next summer.（未来進行形）

c. I (will finish, will have finished) my assignment by noon.（未来完了形）

[Ⅲ] 以下の英文の意味の違いを考えて説明してみよう。

a. I will read the book this week.

b. I've read the book this week.

c. I've been reading the book this week.

Before you read

運動会は好きでしたか？好きだった、または、好きではなかった理由は何でしょうか？

Did you like the *undokai*? _____

Why?: _____

次にグループをつくり、みんなの考えを表にしてみよう。

友人の名前	運動会は好きだった？	理由

Read and Think

|10|

What school event did you like best? One of the most popular days is probably the *undokai*, or sports festival. It is usually held in spring or fall once a year. This custom began many years ago and is unique to Japanese elementary and secondary schools. Ask your parents or adults around you about their memories of the sports festival. Many of them will remember that they were very excited on this day.

At the *undokai*, school children are divided into two or three teams and compete in several activities, including running races and the tug of war. Parents and neighbors come to cheer for the children. They all enjoy this daylong festival very much.

Students in Japan and Western countries learn similar subjects like math and science, but they have very different school events. Why not ask a foreign friend about the school events that they enjoyed most?

(1) Answer the questions.

1. When did the custom of the *undokai* start?

   _____

2. Do schools in other countries have the *undokai*?

   _____

3. What activities does the *undokai* have?

   _____

4. Why do neighbors come to the *undokai*?

   _____

(2) Grammar hunting.

英文から過去形を使っている文を 3 文抜き出し、使われている過去形の動詞を丸で囲みましょう。

1. _____

2. _____

3. _____

(3) What do you think?

今、マラウイやセネガルといった発展途上国で、JICA（国際協力機構）の海外協力隊員は「UNDOKAI」を広げようとしています。彼らはなぜ世界で「UNDOKAI」を開催しようと考えたのでしょうか？運動会から学べることは何か考えてみましょう。

Active Plus

◇部活動も日本の学校に特有な活動の一つです。以下の意見について、あなたは賛成ですか、反対ですか。また、その理由は何ですか？

Opinion: Every school student must belong to a club.

Your opinion: Agree / Disagree

Reason: _____

友人の名前	Agree or Disagree	Reason

◇あなたの考えと友人の考えを比べて異なる点やその理由などについて意見交換してみよう。

Reflection

この課で学んだことを評価しよう。

トピックのCan-do			1		2		3		4		5	
文法の Can-do	理解	1	2	3	4	5	活用	1	2	3	4	5
コメント												

1. Harmony Day は何の日？

　　a. 民族や文化の多様性を祝う日　　b. 合唱コンクールを行う日　　c. 創立記念日

2. この行事が行われる国は？

　　a. Indonesia　　b. Portugal　　c. Australia

5 Chapter

TOPIC **Eating in Japan**
バラエティに富む日本の食事

GRAMMAR 助動詞

Vocabulary

単語の確認をしよう。(**I know** ☑, **I don't know** ?)

1. ☐ branch (　)　　2. ☐ chain (　)　　3. ☐ serve (　)　　4. ☐ specialize (　)
5. ☐ authentic (　)　6. ☐ cuisine (　)　7. ☐ dish (　)　8. ☐ recipe (　)
9. ☐ prepare (　)　10. ☐ ingredient (　)

a. 専門にする	b. 用意する	c. 料理	d. 材料	e. 調理法
f. 真正の	g. チェーン店	h. 一皿	i. 支店	j. 給仕する

🎧 |11| Listen and fill in the blanks.

1. 日本ではお米が主食です。
   Rice is a staple (　　　　) in Japan.

2. いろいろな種類の豆腐が日本料理に使われています。
   Many (　　　　) of tofu are used in Japanese (　　　　).

3. うどんは太くて白い麺ですが、そばは細くて茶色です。
   Udon are (　　　　) white noodles, while soba are (　　　　) and brown.

4. お寿司と刺身の違いをご存知ですか。
   Do you know the (　　　　) (　　　　) sushi and sashimi?

5. 日本の緑茶は私にとって苦すぎます。
   Japanese green tea is too (　　　　) for me.

6. 焼き鳥と焼きそばは日本のお祭りで人気の食べ物です。
   Grilled (　　　　) on bamboo sticks and noodles cooked with pork and
   (　　　　) are popular foods at many festivals in Japan.

🎧 |12| Listen, complete the dialogue and interact.

1. A: Is there a good place to eat dinner with my family near here?
   B: _____

2. A: Have you ever been to this restaurant before?
   B: _____

3. A: I don't have much time, but I'm really hungry. Where should I go?
   B: _____

4. A: There is a line of people waiting outside the restaurant. What should we do?
   B: _____

5. A: I don't really like fish, so can we go to a different restaurant?
   B: _____

GRAMMAR 助動詞

一般に助動詞と呼ばれるものは厳密には will/would, may/might, must, can/could, shall/should などの法助動詞（modal auxiliary）のことです。いずれも助動詞は通常は動詞の前に置かれて、動詞にいろいろな意味を添えます。助動詞は多くの場合 (1) 対人関係と (2) 命題の判断の二通りの意味で使われます。どちらの意味で使われるかは文脈によって判断することになります。

[I] 助動詞が含まれている以下の英文 a~e は（　　）内のどの意味で使われているか考えてみよう。

a.　It will snow tomorrow.（依頼、予想）

b.　May I cancel the schedule?（許可、可能性）

c.　Could I have another cup of tea?（依頼、可能性）

d.　You should see a doctor as soon as possible.（義務、助言、妥当性）

e.　The rumor must be true.（義務、命令、必然性）

[II] 以下の a~d の英文が日本語の意味に合うように（　　）の語句のどちらかを選んで言ってみよう。

a.　(Could, Should) you tell me how to cook sukiyaki?
　　すき焼きの料理の仕方を教えてくれませんか？

b.　I (must, will) leave now. I have to prepare for the exam.
　　もうおいとましなければなりません。試験の準備がありますので。

c.　You (should, should have) come with us. It was a wonderful party.
　　ご一緒するべきでした。素晴らしいパーティでしたよ。

d.　I didn't know your phone number, otherwise I (should, would) have called you.
　　あなたの電話番号がわかりませんでした。知っていたら電話したのに。

[III] 以下の英文はどのような場面で使うのでしょうか。どちらにも must が使われていますが、なぜなのか考えて説明してみよう。

a.　You must visit us when you come to Japan next time.

b.　If you don't have any urgent business, you must have dinner with us.

Before you read

以下の食べ物について、外国人がどう思うか自分の考えを数字で書き入れてみよう。

1. とても人気がある	2. 人気がある	3. あまり人気がない	4. 全然人気がない

1.　(　　) Hamburgers
2.　(　　) Sushi
3.　(　　) *Okonomiyaki*
4.　(　　) *Wagashi* (Japanese sweets)

次にグループをつくり、みんなの考えを表にしてみよう。

友人の名前	1問	2問	3問	4問

|13| 🎧 **Read and Think**

In any city in Japan, you will see branches of international chain restaurants, and also convenience stores offering a variety of snacks and meals. Japan has its own national restaurant chains too. Some of these specialize in Western-style foods like hamburgers, pizza, and sandwiches. However, you can also enjoy authentic Japanese cuisine with the convenience of fast food.

Sushi, tempura and ramen are known all over the world. These dishes are served not only here in Japan, but also in many other countries. For a new experience, you should visit a *yakiniku* (grilled meat) restaurant for the chance to cook your own dinner over a hot grill in the middle of your table. If you enjoy this, you might try *okonomiyaki*, which is like an omelet or pancake. It is often prepared by the customers themselves, so they may choose their own ingredients and toppings.

(1) 次の文が本文の内容に合っている場合にはTを、合っていない場合にはFを選んでみよう。

1. You can find many things to eat in a Japanese convenience store. （ T F ）
2. Authentic Japanese food is less convenient than fast food. （ T F ）
3. You have to visit Japan if you want to try tempura. （ T F ）
4. Going to a *yakiniku* restaurant may be a new experience for foreign visitors.

 （ T F ）
5. When you eat at an *okonomiyaki* restaurant, the chef will cook the ingredients and toppings that you choose. （ T F ）

(2) Grammar hunting.
助動詞を探して下線を引いてみよう。

(3) What do you think?
初めて日本を訪問する人に、あなたなら何を食べるように勧めますか？また、なぜそれを勧めようと思いますか？

🌸 18

Active Plus

◇パートナーと組んで、二人とも行ったことのあるレストランについて考えてみよう。メニューをネットで探すか、注文した料理を思い出してみよう。

Restaurant name: _____

◇以下の項目のそれぞれに点数（1〜10）をつけてみよう。

	My scores:	Partner's scores:	Friends' scores:				
			1	2	3	4	5
Variety	_____ points	_____ points					
Price	_____ points	_____ points					
Convenience	_____ points	_____ points					
Healthiness	_____ points	_____ points					
Uniqueness	_____ points	_____ points					

◇パートナーと分かれて、別の友人にそのレストランについてどう思うか、どのように評価したか尋ねて上の表に記入しよう。5人の友人に聞いてから、元のパートナーのところに戻り、集めた情報を共有しよう。

◇調査した結果を提示し、そのレストランを勧めるか勧めないか、その理由を説明しよう。

Reflection

この課で学んだことを評価しよう。

トピックのCan-do		1	2	3	4	5					
文法の Can-do	理解	1	2	3	4	5	活用	1	2	3	4	5
コメント											

どんな食べ物？ どこの国民食？

1. Meat pie
2. Kebab
3. Poutine
4. Peking duck
5. Crepes

a. China
b. Canada
c. France
d. Australia, New Zealand
e. Turkey

6 Chapter

TOPIC Sightseeing
日本の忍者は大人気

GRAMMAR 名詞

Vocabulary

単語の確認をしよう。(I know ☑, I don't know ?)

1. ☐ appear (　) 　 2. ☐ attraction (　) 　 3. ☐ belief (　) 　 4. ☐ local (　)
5. ☐ master (　) 　 6. ☐ needle (　) 　 7. ☐ practice (　) 　 8. ☐ originate (　)
9. ☐ prefecture (　) 　 10. ☐ region (　)

a. 達人	b. 由来する	c. 針	d. 地域の	e. 信念
f. 県	g. 登場する	h. 呼び物	i. 地域	j. 実践する

🎧 |14| Listen and fill in the blanks.

1. 多くの外国人観光客が伝統的な風俗習慣に関心があります。
   Many foreign (　　　　) are interested in traditional manners and customs.

2. この町では忍者の実演を見ることができます。
   You can see a (　　　　) by a *ninja* in this town.

3. 黒装束の二人の男が塀の上を走って行きます。
   Two men in (　　　　) are running on the fence.

4. 忍者の衣装を着てみることができます。
   You can wear (　　　　) of *ninja*.

5. 阿波踊りは、毎年夏にたくさんの観光客を呼び寄せます。
   Awaodori (　　　　) many visitors every summer.

6. この店ではうどんの作り方を教えてくれます。
   They teach us (　　　　) to make *udon* at this restaurant.

7. 書道を体験してみるのはどうですか？
   How about trying (　　　　)?

🎧 |15| Listen, complete the dialogue and interact.

1. A: When is the best season to travel in Japan?
   B: _____

2. A: I want to climb Mt. Fuji. When is it possible?
   B: _____

3. A: How do you use the square cloth called a "*furoshiki*"?
   B: _____

4. A: What is the small white dome in this picture?
   B: _____

GRAMMAR 名詞

名詞（noun）は、数えられる名詞と数えられない名詞に大別できます。数えられる名詞には普通名詞（store, city など）と集合名詞（family, committee など）があります。数えられる名詞には、単数の場合には冠詞の the, a (an) や this, one などがつき、通常は何もつかないということはありません。複数の場合には、特定のものに限定する the などをつけ、限定しない場合には何もつけません。集合名詞には、集合体を 1 つとしてみる場合とその構成員をみる場合とがあります。

    a. My family is large.

    b. My family are all fine.

数えられない名詞には物質名詞（air, water など）と抽象名詞（honesty, love など）と固有名詞（Ichiro, Ueno Park など）があります。数えられない名詞は、通常は、冠詞の a もつかず、複数形にもなりません。

[I] 以下の a ~ e の英文が日本語の意味に合うように（　　　）に適当な名詞を入れてみよう。

    a.   Thank you for your (　　　　　　).

        親切にしていただいてありがとうございます。

    b.   May I have a (　　　　　　) of (　　　　　　), please?

        水を一杯お願いします。

    c.   Our (　　　　　　) are playing well.

        私たちのチームはよくやっています。

    d.   You can see an old (　　　　　　) over the (　　　　　　).

        橋の向こうに古城が見えます。

    e.   (　　　　　　) is the best (　　　　　　).

        正直は最善の策。

[II] 以下の英文の（　　）の語句のどちらかを選んで正しい英文を作り、それぞれの意味を言ってみよう。

    a.   Consult several (dictionary, dictionaries) for the meaning of this word.

    b.   Do you have any (mean, means) to contact her?

    c.   I appreciate you giving me a lot of (advice, advices).

    d.   For more (information, informations), please contact our office.

    e.   Takayama is famous for its traditional (furniture, furnitures).

[III] 次の対話文の空所に適当な冠詞を入れ、冠詞の用法について説明してみよう。

Mai: I have (　　　　) traditional musical instrument in this case. Look, this is (　　　　) instrument.

Tom: What's it called?

Mai: It's a *wadaiko*.

以下の項目を読み、どう思うか数字を書き入れてみよう。

> 1. ぜひ体験したいと思う　2. 少しそう思う　3. あまりそう思わない　4. 体験したいとは思わない

1. (　) Wearing kimono and going shopping.
2. (　) Riding in a rickshaw.
3. (　) Teaching foreigners how to write *kanji*.
4. (　) Teaching foreigners how to make *origami*.

次にグループを作り、みんなの考えを表にしてみよう。

友人の名前	1問	2問	3問	4問

|16| **Read and Think**

　　How much do you know about *ninja*? Most people will only see *ninja* when they appear on television. You may laugh at the idea, but many foreign people imagine that *ninja* are still common in Japan, and can walk on water and swim under the water for many hours. If you try to find a *ninja* master on the Internet, you will find Kawakami Jinichi. He has been called the last *ninja* master. He is said to have started his *ninja* lessons at the age of six, and has the ability to hear a needle drop in the next room and to disappear in a cloud of smoke.

(1) 次の文が本文の内容に合っている場合にはTを、合っていない場合にはFを選んでみよう。

1. You can see *ninja* on television.　　　　　　　　　　　　　　　　（ T　F ）
2. Many foreign people think *ninja* are fiction.　　　　　　　　　　（ T　F ）
3. Kawakami Jinichi is a living master of *ninja*.　　　　　　　　　　（ T　F ）
4. Many foreign tourists know that he uses fake skills.　　　　　　　（ T　F ）

(2) Grammar hunting.

　　数えられない名詞を探し出してみよう。辞書で確認するのも良い方法です。

(3) What do you think?

　　日本の忍者はなぜ生まれたのだと思いますか？みんなで話し合ってみよう。

Active Plus

◇ 日本文化の体験を誘うチラシを見つけました。あなたはどちらを体験したいですか？

A *mikoshi* or a portable shrine is a popular part of the city festival. Why don't you join us and enjoy carrying a *mikoshi*? The experience will be lots of fun! Costumes for the festival can be borrowed from the shrine office.

Zazen originated in India and was introduced to Japan through China. It is a form of mental or spiritual training. Now you can enjoy *zazen* in some temples. If you would like to experience it, you can ask at a temple and find out whether you can try it.

◇同様に日本文化の体験を誘う企画を立ててみよう。上記と同様に誘いの英文とさし絵を考えよう。

Reflection

この課で学んだことを評価しよう。

トピックのCan-do		1		2		3		4		5	
文法の Can-do	理解	1	2	3	4	5	活用	1	2	3	4	5
コメント											

 World Quiz

1. この家は何と呼ばれるでしょうか？
   a. Ger   b. White House   c. Moving Home

2. どこの国にあるでしょうか？
   a. Sudan   b. Mongolia   c. Argentina

7
Chapter

TOPIC **Ancient Agriculture**
伝統に根ざした日本の農業

GRAMMAR 準動詞：不定詞・動名詞

Vocabulary

単語の確認をしよう。(**I know** ☑, **I don't know** ?)

1. □surround (　) 　2. □ancient (　) 　3. □village (　) 　　4. □particular (　)
5. □common (　) 　6. □form (　) 　　7. □agricultural (　) 　8. □product (　)
9. □harvest (　) 　10. □nowadays (　)

a. 形成する	b. 農業の	c. 村	d. 古代の	e. 囲む
f. 特殊の	g. 収穫する	h. 産物	i. 共通の	j. このごろは

🎧|17| Listen and fill in the blanks.

1. 日本は海に囲まれています。

   Japan is (　　　　) by the (　　　　).

2. 日本の農夫達はよく米を生産していました。

   Japanese (　　　　) were likely to produce (　　　　).

3. 村人達は集まってグループで一緒に働きました。

   People in their (　　　　) gathered and worked (　　　　) in groups.

4. 彼等は秋に米を収穫しなければなりませんでした。

   They had to (　　　　) rice in the (　　　　).

5. 彼らは他の農産物も生産しました。

   They (　　　　) other agricultural (　　　　), (　　　　).

🎧|18| Listen, complete the dialogue and interact.

1. A: How often do you eat rice?

   B: _____

2. A: Are you interested in farming history in Japan? Why or why not?

   B: _____

3. A: What do you think about Japanese farmers?

   B: _____

4. A: What is a merit of Japanese farming?

   B: _____

GRAMMAR 準動詞：不定詞・動名詞

不定詞 (infinitive)（to+動詞の原形）には、名詞的用法、副詞的用法、形容詞的用法があります。不定詞のtoは前置詞のtoと同様に「どこどこへ向かう、気持ちが向いている」という原義があります。たとえば、I want to be an interpreter. というのは通訳になるという方向に気持ちが向いている、ということです。名詞的用法の場合には、名詞と同様の働きをするので、主語や補語や目的語になります。

動名詞 (gerund)（動詞＋ing）は文字通り動詞と名詞の両方の働きをします。したがって、動名詞や動名詞句は主語や補語や目的語になります。

[Ⅰ] 以下のa～dの英文が日本語の意味に合うように（　　）に適当な不定詞を入れ、それぞれどのような用法か答えてみよう。

a. It is interesting (　　　　　) rice-planting. （＿＿＿的用法）
田植えの体験は面白いです。

b. Last week we went hiking (　　　　) terraced paddy fields. （＿＿＿的用法）
先週私たちは棚田を見にハイキングに出かけました。

c. Do you have anything (　　　　) for lunch? （＿＿＿的用法）
お昼に食べるものを何か持っていますか？

d. I want (　　　　) a farmer using no chemicals. （＿＿＿的用法）
私は農薬を使わない農家になりたいです。

[Ⅱ] 以下の英文の（　）の語句のどちらかを選んで正しい英文を作り、それぞれの意味を言ってみよう。（　）内のどちらとも可能な場合もあります。

a. They usually finish (to work, working) outdoors before dark.
b. He hoped (to make, making) his country rich
c. She went out without (to say, saying) a word.
d. We enjoyed (to dig, digging) up potatoes.
e. I like (to cook, cooking) *nikujaga* or meat and potatoes.

[Ⅲ] 以下の2つの英文の意味の違いを考えて言ってみよう。

a. I remember to give her a phone call.
b. I remember giving her a phone call.

それぞれの項目を読み、どう思うか数字を書き入れてみよう。

1. そう思う	2. 少しそう思う	3. あまりそう思わない	4. そう思わない

1. (　) It is important for Japanese people to meet their common needs in their own community.

2. (　) Japanese people tend to do things at their own pace.

3. (　) In order to cooperate as a group, people need to make decisions slowly.

4. (　) Working together involves difficult tasks.

次にグループをつくり、みんなの考えを表にしてみよう。

友人の名前	1問	2問	3問	4問

|19| **Read and Think**

As a result of being surrounded by the ocean, Japanese farmers developed particular ways of living in their ancient societies. They were most likely to produce rice as their main product. It took a lot of time and effort to plant and grow rice from seeds, so people in their villages gathered and worked together in groups. They did the same thing when they had to harvest rice in the autumn. In order to work as a group, they had to develop common goals, which usually took a long time. However, once they formed these goals and could work together well, they were likely to move forward to make other agricultural products. The style of farming has changed nowadays, but the group-minded spirit of people is still alive.

(1) 次の文が本文の内容に合っている場合にはTを、合っていない場合にはFを選んでみよう。

1. Japanese farmers tended to make rice as their main product. （ T　F ）
2. Japanese farmers easily planted and grew rice from seeds. （ T　F ）
3. People worked individually in Japanese communities. （ T　F ）
4. Japanese farmers had to develop common goals. （ T　F ）
5. Present-day Japanese farmers do not think highly of working in groups. （ T　F ）

(2) Grammar hunting.

不定詞と動名詞を含んだ文を探してみよう。

(3) What do you think?

"Japanese people have to make common goals in their community" という行為をどのように思いますか？また、なぜそう思いますか？

Active Plus

近年、日本の地方の農村・漁村に宿泊するファームステイ（農山漁村滞在型旅行）が外国人観光客に人気になってきています。

◇ファームステイとは何か調べ、なぜ人気なのか考えてみよう。

_____

_____

◇ファームステイでどのような体験をすることができるのかリストアップし、ファームステイの魅力を伝える英語の紹介文を作ってみよう。

_____

_____

◇海外でのファームステイも人気です。どんなファームステイがあるのかネットで調べて、英語で友人に伝えてみよう。

_____

_____

Reflection

この課で学んだことを評価しよう。

トピックのCan-do				1		2		3		4		5	
文法の Can-do	理解	1	2	3	4	5	活用	1	2	3	4	5	
コメント													

ケニアの環境保護活動家のワンガリ・マータイさんが世界に広めた日本語は何？

1. Sho-ene　　2. Setsuyaku　　3. Mottainai

8 Chapter

TOPIC **Politics**

日本の政治のしくみ

GRAMMAR 能動態・受動態

Vocabulary

単語の確認をしよう。(**I know** ☑ , **I don't know** ?)

1. □ principle (　) 　　2. □ Diet (　) 　　3. □ mayor (　) 　　4. □ governor (　)
5. □ democracy (　) 　6. □ pacifism (　) 　7. □ emperor (　)
8. □ constitution (　) 　9. □ government (　) 　10. □ sovereignty (　)

a. 民主主義	b. 知事	c. 国会	d. 平和主義	e. 天皇
f. 市長	g. 憲法	h. 原則	i. 政治・政府	j. 主権

|20| ### Listen and fill in the blanks.

1. 人種差別はいかなる場合でも禁じられなければなりません。
   Racial discrimination is (　　　　　) in any situation.

2. 生存権は憲法で保障されています。
   The right of life is (　　　　　) by the constitution.

3. 日本の政治は民主主義に基づいています。
   The government of Japan is (　　　　　) on democracy.

4. 通りにゴミを捨てると罰せられます。
   You are (　　　　　) for throwing away trash on the street.

5. 運転免許は運転試験に合格した人に付与されます。
   A driving license is (　　　　　) to those who (　　　　　) the driving test.

6. 最近ではユニバーサルデザインが多くの場所で使われるようになりました。
   Recently universal designs have (　　　　　) (　　　　　) in many places.

7. 交番は駅前や街角によく見られます。
   Police boxes (　　　　　) often (　　　　　) in front of the station and on the corner of the street.

|21| ### Listen, complete the dialogue and interact.

1. A: Is high school included in compulsory education?
   B: _____

2. A: Does Japan have a draft system?
   B: _____

3. A: Can you vote directly for the prime minister in Japan?
   B: _____

4. A: Is spitting on the road allowed in Japan?
   B: _____

28

GRAMMAR 能動態・受動態

英語の文には能動態 (active voice) の文と受動態 (passive voice) の文があります。受動態は主語＋be動詞＋動詞の過去分詞で構成されます。また、動詞が表す行為の主体を明確にしたいときにはbyを使って by someoneのように言います。能動態の文と受動態の文は概念的には同じ意味であっても、ニュアンスが異なることもあります。

[I] 以下のa～eの英文を（　　　）内の指示に従って書き換えてみよう。

a.　All of us must follow this rule.（this rule を主語に）

_____

b.　They serve Japanese food at this restaurant.（Japanese food を主語に）

_____

c.　He showed me the way to the police box.（me を主語に）

_____

d.　You should not tell your address to anyone you don't know.
　　（your address を主語に）

_____

e.　I was made happy by your words.（your words を主語に）

_____

[II] 以下のa～eの英文が日本語の意味に合うように（　　　）の 語句のどちらかを選んで言ってみよう。

a.　Walking on the escalator is not (recommend, recommended).
　　エスカレーターで歩くことは勧められません。

b.　The right to vote for the captain (gives, is given) to everyone in the team.
　　チームのキャプテンを選ぶ選挙権はチームの全員に与えられています。

c.　You must (obtain, be obtained) all the credits needed for graduation.
　　卒業するには必要なすべての単位を取得しなくてはなりません。

d.　Your passport must (carry, be carried) with you when going abroad.
　　外国に出かけるときにはパスポートを携行しなければなりません。

e.　You'll see guide boards (write, written) in several languages in the station.
　　駅には複数言語で表示された案内板があります。

[III] 能動態と受動態の文を使うときには前後のコンテキストに留意する必要があります。次の質問に対する応答としてはａｂのどちらがふさわしいでしょうか？

What did volunteers do along the street?

a.　They planted flowers.

b.　Flowers were planted by them.

Before you read

以下の項目が正しいと思えばTを、正しくないと思えばFを（　　）に入れよう。答えを友達と確認してみよう。

1. （　　） The Japanese constitution defines the emperor as a symbol of the nation.
2. （　　） The Diet of Japan consists of two houses.
3. （　　） The term of the House of Representatives is six years.
4. （　　） The ministers are chosen by the emperor.
5. （　　） Japanese people can become candidates for the Diet at the age of twenty.

|22| Read and Think

The Diet of Japan consists of two chambers, the House of Representatives and the House of Councilors. The Diet selects the prime minister, and other State ministers are appointed by the prime minister. Members of the Diet, prefectural governors, mayors of the cities, towns, and villages, and the assembly members are elected directly. The right to vote is given to all Japanese men and women who have reached the age of 18. To be elected as a prefectural governor or to the House of Councilors, one must be at least 30 years old. The minimum age to run for other offices is 25.

(1) Answer the questions.

1. What are the two chambers of the Diet?

_____

2. Is the prime minister of Japan elected directly?

_____

3. How are the State ministers chosen?

_____

4. When do people have the right to vote?

_____

(2) Grammar hunting.

受動態の文を見つけてみよう。

(3) What do you think?

日本の民主主義を支える最も重要な法律は憲法です。その憲法を支える3つの原則は何でしょうか。

Active Plus

◇成人になるのはいつから？

The minimum age for voting was lowered from 20 to 18. Following from this policy, some people say that Japanese people should be regarded as adults when they reach the age of 18, and allowed not only to vote but also to drink and smoke. What do you think of this opinion?

◇この考えのメリットとデメリットを挙げて話し合ってみよう。

Merits: _____

Demerits: _____

◇あなたの考えまたはグループの考えを英語で発表してみよう。

_____

_____

_____

Reflection

この課で学んだことを評価しよう。

トピックのCan-do				1	2	3	4	5			
文法の Can-do	理解	1	2	3	4	5	活用	1	2	3	4	5
コメント											

「チューインガムを食べてはいけない」国はどこ？

1. United Kingdom   2. Switzerland   3. Singapore

9 Chapter

TOPIC **Economy**
時代を映す日本経済

GRAMMAR 接続詞：等位接続詞

Vocabulary

単語の確認をしよう。(**I know** ☑, **I don't know** ？)

1. □ pension ( ) 　2. □ industry ( ) 　3. □ workforce ( ) 　4. □ income ( )
5. □ investment ( ) 　6. □ tax ( ) 　7. □ consumption ( )
8. □ employment ( ) 　9. □ competition ( ) 　10. □ security ( )

a. 労働力	b. 収入	c. 投資	d. 保障	e. 競争
f. 消費	g. 雇用	h. 税	i. 年金	j. 産業

|23| Listen and fill in the blanks.

1. 経済的な落ち込みに伴って、奨学金とアルバイトに頼る学生が多くなっています。
   (　　　) the economy declines, a lot of students depend on scholarships
   (　　　) part-time jobs.

2. 日本の高度経済成長期には終身雇用制度が重要な役割を果たしていましたが、近年ではこの制度は以前
   ほど一般的ではなくなってきています。
   The lifetime employment system played an important role at the time of
   Japan's high economic growth period, (　　　) in recent years this system is
   less popular (　　　) it used to be.

3. 直接税は収入に対して、間接税は消費と他の支出に対して課されます。
   Direct taxes are imposed on income (　　　) indirect taxes are imposed on
   consumption (　　　) other expenditures.

4. 高齢人口が増加し、若年齢世代は将来の年金に向けて支払う額がますます多くなるでしょう。
   The population has been increasingly aging, (　　　) the younger generation
   will have to pay more (　　　) more for the pension scheme in the future.

5. 出来る時にお金を貯めておきましょう。そうしないと将来苦労することになるでしょう。
   Save your money (　　　) you can, (　　　) you will go through hardships in
   the future.

|24| Listen, complete the dialogue and interact.

1. A: How many credit cards do you have?
   B: _____

2. A: Do you think more foreign workers are needed in Japan? If so, why?
   B: _____

3. A: What percentage of Japanese workers do you think are engaged in primary industries?

    B: _____

4. A: Are there any special products or industries in your town?

    B: _____

GRAMMAR　接続詞：等位接続詞

文と文とを連結する最も一般的な方法は、接続詞 (conjunction) を用いることです。接続詞はその接続の仕方によって等位接続と従位接続に分けられます。前者は節（主語と述語が含まれるもの）と節が対等の関係で結ばれる接続をいい、後者は一方の節が他方に従属する、つまり主節と従節の関係になるような接続をいいます。後者については次章で取り上げます。等位接続詞の代表的なものは and, but, or です。

[Ⅰ] 以下のa～dの英文が日本語の意味に合うように（　　）に適当な接続詞を入れてみよう。

  a.　I don't have much money, (　　　　) I live very happily.
     私にはお金はあまりありませんが、楽しく暮らしています。

  b.　You can pay by cash (　　　　) you can use a credit card.
     現金で支払うこともできますが、クレジットカードを使うこともできます。

  c.　Bring your own shopping bag with you, (　　　　) reduce the use of plastic bags.
     買い物袋を持参してプラスチックバッグの使用を減らしましょう。

  d.　I didn't waste my time when I was young, (　　　　) studied hard every day.
     私は若いころは時間を無駄にせずに毎日勉強しました。

[Ⅱ] 以下の英文の（　　）の語のいずれかを選んで英文を完成し、それぞれの意味を言ってみよう。

  a.　One type of accommodation in Japan is the Western style hotel, (and, or) another is the traditional Japanese style inn called a *ryokan*.

  b.　In Japan there is no custom of tipping, (but, so) you don't have to give a tip to your taxi driver.

  c.　Many tourists are enjoying themselves, (and, but, or) at least they appear to be.

[Ⅲ] 以下の英文 a. b. c. で使われているandは以下のどのような関係を示すために使われているか考えてみよう。

1. 因果関係	2. 対比	3. 肯定条件

  a.　My elder sister is reserved *and* my younger sister is aggressive.　　(　　)
  b.　Give me some time *and* I'll find the answer to this question.　　(　　)
  c.　I heard an explosion *and* phoned the police.　　(　　)

Before you read

以下の項目を読み、どう思うか数字を書き入れてみよう。

1. そう思う	2. 少しそう思う	3. あまりそう思わない	4. そう思わない

1. (　) Japanese people like saving money.
2. (　) Part-time jobs are important for society.
3. (　) When shopping, I like to pay by credit card rather than by cash.
4. (　) Consumption tax in Japan is too high.

次にグループをつくり、みんなの考えを表にしてみよう。

友人の名前	1問	2問	3問	4問

|25| Read and Think

　　"Convenience" is a keyword in describing life in Japan. You will find convenience stores on almost any street in a city or town. Many of these stores serve customers 24 hours a day, and they stay open even on public holidays. You can choose from a range of foods and drinks at a convenience store or find a nearby vending machine to buy what you need. In Japan, these machines sell not only drinks but also snacks, newspapers, and many other products. There are millions of vending machines all around the country, and they help us to live more comfortable lives.

(1) 次の文が本文の内容に合っている場合にはTを、合っていない場合にはFを選んでみよう。

1. Most convenience stores are located only along the main streets.　　(　T　F　)
2. Many convenience stores close on public holidays.　　(　T　F　)
3. Vending machines sell many daily goods as well as drinks.　　(　T　F　)
4. Vending machines contribute little to our lives.　　(　T　F　)

(2) Grammar hunting.
　　等位接続詞が使われている文を見つけてみよう。

(3) What do you think?

　日本にはなぜ自動販売機が多くあるのでしょうか？理由を考えてみよう。

Active Plus

食料は生活を維持するための基本です。日本では農業生産者の高齢化や食料自給率（food self-sufficiency rate）の低さが問題になっています。今後も安全で十分な食料を確保していくために最も大事だと思う方策を提案しよう。

◇食料自給率が低い原因を考えて書き出してみよう。

_____

_____

◇食料自給率を上げる方策を考えて書き出してみよう。

_____

_____

◇自給率が低い原因と解決策を盛り込んだ英文を書いて発表しよう。

_____

_____

Reflection

この課で学んだことを評価しよう。

トピックのCan-do				1		2		3		4		5	
文法の Can-do	理解	1	2	3	4	5	活用	1	2	3	4	5	
コメント													

この通貨はどこの国のもの？

1. Rupiah　　2. Real　　3. Birr

a. Ethiopia　　b. Indonesia　　c. Brazil

TOPIC Sports
大会を盛り上げるサポーター

GRAMMAR 接続詞：従位接続詞

Vocabulary

単語の確認をしよう。(**I know** ☑, **I don't know** ？)

1. ☐politeness (　)　　**2.** ☐reporter (　)　**3.** ☐outcome (　)　**4.** ☐discourage (　)
5. ☐gather (　)　　　　**6.** ☐astonish (　)　**7.** ☐influence (　)　**8.** ☐improve (　)
9. ☐atmosphere (　)　**10.** ☐trash (　)

a. 結果	b. 集める	c. 記者	d. 礼儀正しさ	e. 改善する
f. 落胆させる	g. ゴミ	h. 雰囲気	i. 影響を与える	j. 驚かせる

🎧26 Listen and fill in the blanks.

1. 日本人のサポーターは記者たちを驚かせました。

   Japanese (　　　　　) astonished (　　　　　) reporters.

2. 日本のチームは試合の初めにはリードしていました。

   The Japanese (　　　　　) took the (　　　　　) at the start of their game.

3. 彼らは試合の結果にかなり失望しました。

   They were very (　　　　　) with the game (　　　　　).

4. 日本人のファンはゴミを集めました。

   Japanese (　　　　　) gathered (　　　　　).

5. 彼らは前向きな態度を保ちました。

   They (　　　　　) a positive (　　　　　).

🎧27 Listen, complete the dialogue and interact.

1. A: Do you think that politeness is important in sports? Why or why not?

   B: _____

2. A: Do you watch sport on TV in your free time? Why or why not?

   B: _____

3. A: Can I play soccer after I finish my homework?

   B: _____

4. A: Although I am not good at basketball, I can play soccer. How about you?

   B: _____

5. A: What should I do if there is no direct flight to Brazil?

   B: _____

GRAMMAR 接続詞：従位接続詞

接続関係で、一方が他方の主従関係になるような接続を従位接続と言います。たとえば、以下の文を見てみよう。

Kazu became a famous soccer player after he returned from Brazil.
　　　　　　A　　　　　　　　　　　　　　　B

この文は2つの節からなっています。Bの節はそれだけでは文として成り立たないので従位節（従属節）と言います。一方、Aの節はこれだけでも文として成り立つので主節と言います。このような従位節を導く接続詞を従位接続詞と言います。接続詞の意味や接続の仕方によって、時、原因、理由、場所、目的、条件などの様々な意味を表します。

[Ⅰ] 以下のa~dの英文が日本語の意味に合うように（　　）に適当な接続詞（接続表現）を選び文を完成させよう。

as	while	till	as if

a.　(　　　　) I was jogging, I lost a contact lens.
　　ジョギングを している間にコンタクトレンズを落としてしまいました。

b.　(　　　　) you know, Naomi is the best tennis player in Japan.
　　ご存じのようにナオミは日本で一番のテニスプレイヤーです。

c.　He talks (　　　) he knew everything about judo.
　　彼は柔道のことなら何でも知っているかのように話します。

d.　They played baseball (　　　) it got dark.
　　彼らは暗くなるまで野球をしていました。

[Ⅱ] 以下の英文の（　　）内の接続詞のどちらかを選んで英文を完成し、それぞれの意味を言ってみよう。

a.　(As far as, Since) I know, she is practicing kendo in the gym.

b.　(Although, Because) he started playing wheelchair basketball only two years ago, he is now the ace of our team.

c.　We are training before school, (because, before) we are going to participate in the fall tournament.

d.　(If, Since) the circumstances permit, please join our team.

[Ⅲ] 以下の英文の（　　）内に適当な表現を入れて意味の通る英文を完成させよう。答えが1つとは限りません。

He flunked English. (　　　　　　　) he has to take it again this year.

Before you read

それぞれの項目について自分の考えを数字で書き入れてみよう。

| 1. そう思う 　　　2. 少しそう思う 　　　3. あまりそう思わない 　　　4. そう思わない |

1. (　) Japanese people are polite.
2. (　) Japanese players are well-mannered.
3. (　) Japanese people are kind.
4. (　) Japanese fans are pleased when their opponent's players make mistakes.

次にグループをつくり、みんなの考えを表にしてみよう。

友人の名前	1問	2問	3問	4問

|28| Read and Think

　　The Japanese team took the lead at the start of their soccer game during the 2014 soccer World Cup in Brazil, but lost the game. Although the Japanese fans were very discouraged by the game outcome, they started to gather trash around their seats. This conduct astonished news reporters from all over the world. Now, Japanese soccer fans' politeness has influenced fans of other sports such as baseball, rugby, and figure skating. The example of Japanese sports fans' behavior helps reform and improve the atmosphere at sports competitions.

(1) 次の文が本文の内容に合っている場合にはTを、合っていない場合にはFを選んでみよう。

1. During the soccer World Cup in Brazil, news reporters were surprised at Japanese fans' behavior. 　　　　　　　　　　　　　　　　　　　(T 　F)

2. The Japanese supporters were not discouraged after Japan lost the game. 　　　　　　　　　　　　　　　　　　　　　　　　　　　　　　(T 　F)

3. After the game all soccer fans started to gather trash around their seats. 　　　　　　　　　　　　　　　　　　　　　　　　　　　　　　(T 　F)

4. Japanese fans' politeness influences other sports fans' behavior. 　　(T 　F)

(2) **Grammar hunting.**
　　等位接続詞と従位接続詞を含んだ文がどこにあるか探してみよう。

(3) What do you think?

"Japanese fans started to gather trash around their seats" という行為をどのように思いますか？また、なぜそう思いますか？

Active Plus

最近はボランティア活動に参加する人が多くなってきました。

◇ボランティアの定義をペアやグループで考えて発表してみよう。

_____

_____

◇ボランティアを行う上で日本と他の国で異なる考え方があるかどうか調べてみよう。

_____

_____

◇今後どのようなボランティアが必要になると思いますか。自分が行いたいボランティア活動を考えて英語で言ってみよう。

_____

_____

Reflection

この課で学んだことを評価しよう。

トピックのCan-do				1	2	3	4	5			
文法の Can-do	理解	1	2	3	4	5	活用	1	2	3	4	5
コメント											

soccer の語源・由来は？

1. association football をもとにした造語
2. socks player をもとにした造語
3. soccer を広めた英雄の名前

TOPIC Changes in Japanese Sports
日本人が好きなスポーツ

GRAMMAR 比較：原級比較

Vocabulary

単語の確認をしよう。(**I know** ☑ , **I don't know** ？)

1. ☐ develop ( )　　2. ☐ religious ( )　　3. ☐ national ( )　　4. ☐ spectator ( )
5. ☐ dominate ( )　　6. ☐ current ( )　　7. ☐ achieve ( )　　8. ☐ association ( )
9. ☐ allow ( )　　　10. ☐ stable ( )

a. 協会	b. 風靡する	c. 展開する	d. 部屋	e. 宗教の
f. 果たす	g. 許す	h. 観客	i. 国民・国家の	j. 現在の

|29| Listen and fill in the blanks.

1. 相撲は日本の国技と言われています。
   Sumo is ( ) to be Japan's ( ) sport.

2. 日本は柔道で他の国よりも多くのオリンピックメダルを獲得してきました。
   Japan has won ( ) Olympic medals for judo ( ) any other country.

3. 日本初の本格的な野球チームは1878年に設立されました。
   Japan's first ( ) baseball team was ( ) in 1878.

4. スポーツの日は1964年の東京オリンピックを記念する祝日です。
   Sports Day is a national ( ) that ( ) the 1964 Tokyo Olympics.

5. 第9回のラグビーワールドカップは2019年に日本で開催されました。
   The ( ) Rugby World Cup was ( ) in Japan in 2019.

6. 数百年前から空手はありますが、オリンピック競技になったのは2020年です。
   Although it is ( ) of years old, karate only ( ) an Olympic sport in 2020.

|30| Listen, complete the dialogue and interact.

1. A: What sports did you play in high school?
   B: _____

2. A: Have you ever gone to watch a sumo tournament?
   B: _____

3. A: Do many school students practice sumo wrestling?
   B: _____

4. A: Which sport do you think Japan will win a gold medal for at the Olympics?
   B: _____

GRAMMAR　比較：原級比較

形容詞や副詞を活用して比較の表現を作ることができます。その中で〈as...as〉を用いて2つのものが同程度であること、または倍数であることを述べることを原級比較と言います。否定文のときは〈not as[so]...as〉のようになります。2つのものを比べるという点では比喩も同様です。比喩を上手に活用すると豊かな表現ができるようになります。比喩には〈as...as〉や〈like...〉のような比喩であること示す表現を用いる場合（直喩）と比喩であることを示す表現を用いないで直接その言葉を言ってたとえる場合（隠喩）があります。

［Ⅰ］以下のa～dの英文が日本語の意味に合うように（　　）に適当な形容詞または副詞を入れて文を完成させよう。

a.　Rugby is as (　　　　　) as soccer.
　　　ラグビーはサッカーと同じくらい人気があります。

b.　He can run as (　　　　　) as a horse.
　　　彼は馬と同じくらいの速さで走れます。

c.　This gymnasium is twice as (　　　　　) as the one in my town.
　　　この体育館は私の町の体育館の2倍の大きさです。

d.　Cricket is not played as (　　　　　) as baseball in Japan.
　　　日本ではクリケットは野球ほど行われません。

［Ⅱ］以下の英文の（　　）内のどちらかを選んで英文を完成し、それぞれの意味を言ってみよう。

a.　Rikako swims as (fast, first) as any other swimmer in the world.

b.　*Hagoita* used to be as (popular, known) as badminton.

c.　There are not as (many, much) people who practice *naginata* as there are people who practice kendo.

d.　Our school cheerleading team practices as (far, hard) as the soccer team.

［Ⅲ］以下の日本文の意味を直喩と隠喩を使って英語で表現してみよう。

　「レスリングは私の人生そのものだ。」

Before you read

以下の項目が正しいと思えばTを、正しくないと思えばFを（　　）に入れよう。答えを友達と確認してみよう。

1. （　） The sport of sumo originally came from Mongolia.
2. （　） Sumo is not as popular in Japan as it used to be.
3. （　） Most sumo wrestlers in Japan today were born in other countries.
4. （　） Other countries also have traditional forms of wrestling.
5. （　） Hundreds of wrestlers become *yokozuna* each year.

|31| ## Read and Think

Sumo wrestling developed from ancient Japanese religious customs into a popular spectator sport over 2000 years. Today it is as popular as ever with fans in Japan but is also enjoyed around the world. Even in Japan, the sport is now largely dominated by foreign-born wrestlers. Although they compete using Japanese *shikona* (ring names), several of the current top wrestlers are from Mongolia, where traditional wrestling is as important as in Japan. Over the last 20 years, of the six men who have achieved the title of *yokozuna* (sumo's top rank) only one was born in Japan. Perhaps because of this, the Japan Sumo Association no longer allows as many foreign wrestlers to join each training stable as in the past.

(1) Answer the questions.

1. How long has the sport of sumo been developing?

   _____

2. Has sumo become more or less popular with fans in Japan?

   _____

3. Why are many top sumo wrestlers in Japan from Mongolia?

   _____

4. How many foreign-born wrestlers have become *yokozuna* in the last 20 years?

   _____

(2) Grammar hunting.

原級比較の文を見つけてみよう。

(3) What do you think?

日本相撲協会はもっと外国人力士を増やすべきだと思いますか？ それとも減らすべきだと思いますか？

Active Plus

オリンピックではどのようなスポーツが行われるのでしょうか。

◇オリンピックスポーツのリストをネットで調べ、自分は興味があるが、日本では人気のないスポーツを１つ見つけてみよう。

◇次に、３人または４人でグループになり、あなたが取り上げたスポーツについて、以下の４つの質問をし、答えを表にまとめよう。

The sport I chose: _____	Friends' answers (Yes / No)			
	1	2	3	4
1. Would you like to try it?				
2. Are you interested in watching it?				
3. Do you think Japanese school students should practice it?				
4. Do you think Japan will ever win a gold medal for it?				

◇グループで質問と回答が終わった後、どうしたら日本でそのスポーツが人気になるか、みんなで考えてみよう。

Reflection

この課で学んだことを評価しよう。

トピックの Can-do			1		2		3		4		5		
文法の Can-do	理解	1	2	3	4	5	活用	1	2	3	4	5	
コメント													

どの国でどのスポーツが人気か組み合わせてみよう。

1. United States
2. China
3. India
4. Canada
5. New Zealand
6. United Kingdom
7. Cuba

a. Rugby
b. Soccer
c. Ice hockey
d. Basketball
e. American football
f. Baseball
g. Cricket

TOPIC Favorite Places to visit

お薦め観光地

GRAMMAR 比較：比較級・最上級

Vocabulary

単語の確認をしよう。(**I know** ☑ , **I don't know** ?)

1. ☐ temple (　) 　2. ☐ recommend (　　) 　3. ☐ attractive (　　) 　4. ☐ excellent (　　)

5. ☐ political (　) 　6. ☐ economic (　　) 　7. ☐ shrine (　　) 　8. ☐ elegant (　　)

9. ☐ heritage (　) 　10. ☐ destination (　　)

a. 優れた	b. 遺産	c. 魅力的な	d. 勧める	e. 優雅な
f. 目的地	g. 寺院	h. 政治的な	i. 経済の	j. 神社

🎧 32 Listen and fill in the blanks.

1. 観光客はよく新幹線で日本を周っています。

   Tourists (　　　　　) use the Shinkansen to get (　　　　　) Japan.

2. 富士山は観光客に人気のある目的地です。

   Mt. Fuji is a (　　　　　) destination for tourists.

3. 京都は古代日本において政治の中心地でした。

   Kyoto was the (　　　　　) capital of (　　　　) Japan.

4. 京都では必ずたっぷりと時間を過ごせるようにしましょう。

   Make (　　　　　) you have (　　　　　) time to spend in Kyoto.

5. 日本を旅行する間にほかの多くの場所に行くことができます。

   You can (　　　　　) plenty of other (　　　　　) during your trip to Japan.

🎧 33 Listen, complete the dialogue and interact.

1. A: What sights can you see in Tokyo?

   B: _____

2. A: Which place would you like to visit?

   B: _____

3. A: Could you tell me about Tokyo Skytree?

   B: _____

4. A: What is a commuter pass?

   B: _____

5. A: Why do you use the Shinkansen?

   B: _____

GRAMMAR 比較：比較級・最上級

2つのもののうち、どちらか一方の程度が他方よりも高いか低いかなどを示す場合には、比較級を用いて〈比較級＋than〉で表します。また、3つ以上のものの中で、どれが最も程度が高いか低いとかを示す場合には、最上級で表します。最も程度が高い、または低い、というのは特定のことを指すので定冠詞の the をつけることが多いです。

[Ⅰ] 以下のa～dの英文が日本語の意味に合うように（　）に適当な表現を入れて文を完成させよう。

a. Japan is (　　　　　　) California.
日本はカリフォルニアよりも小さいです。

b. In winter, it is (　　　　　　) in New York (　　　　　　) in Tokyo.
冬のニューヨークは東京よりも寒いです。

c. Is it (　　　　　　) to use the Shinkansen or an airplane to go to Osaka?
大阪へ行くには新幹線と飛行機ではどちらが速いですか？

d. The Shinano River is (　　　　　　) river in Japan.
信濃川は日本で一番長い川です。

[Ⅱ] 以下の英文の（　）内の語句のどちらかを選んで英文を完成し、それぞれの意味を言ってみよう。

a. What is (the largest, the famous) castle in Japan?
b. Which do you like (better, well), Kinkakuji or Ginkakuji ?
c. What is (the best, the most) fruit in Aomori prefecture?
d. This shrine was built (at least, at last) 500 years ago.

[Ⅲ] 以下の英文を比較級で表現するにはどうすれば良いか、ペアで考えて言ってみよう。

Mt. Fuji is the highest mountain in Japan.

Before you read

それぞれの項目について自分の考えを数字で書き入れてみよう。

| 1. そう思う | 2. 少しそう思う | 3. あまりそう思わない | 4. そう思わない |

1. ( ) Many international tourists get around Japan taking a taxi.
2. ( ) Mt. Fuji is the most beautiful mountain in Japan.
3. ( ) Many people like to climb Mt. Fuji early in the morning.
4. ( ) In Kyoto, you can see only old heritage.

次にグループをつくり、みんなの考えを表にしてみよう。

友人の名前	1問	2問	3問	4問

Read and Think

|34|

We recommend riding the Shinkansen when you visit Kyoto using a (*)Japan Rail Pass. Taking the bullet train is one of the fastest and most attractive ways to get to the ancient city. It will take you only a little over two hours from Tokyo. During the journey, you will have an excellent view of Mt. Fuji, which is considered Japan's most beautiful mountain.

Keep travelling west on the train and you will soon reach Kyoto. Kyoto is also known as "*Koto*" (old capital), as the city used to be the political and economic center of Japan. You will have lots of things to do, seeing beautiful temples, shrines and castles, experiencing elegant culture and enjoying excellent cuisine.

* ジャパン・レール・パス:外国人観光客用の格安周遊券

(1) Answer the questions.

1. How long does it take to get from Tokyo to Kyoto?

   _____

2. What can you see during the Shinkansen journey?

   _____

3. Why is Kyoto sometimes called '*Koto*'?

   _____

4. What can you see in Kyoto?

   _____

(2) Grammar hunting.

最上級を用いている文を探してみよう。

(3) What do you think?

北海道も外国人観光客に人気です。北海道へ旅行する時にはどのような交通手段を勧めますか？あなたの考えを上の英文を参考にして英語で言ってみよう。

Active Plus

世界遺産にはたくさんの観光客が訪れます。

◇富士山は世界文化遺産に認定されていて、毎年、多くの外国人が観光に訪れます。なぜ人気があるのか、世界文化遺産に推薦された理由を参考に考えてみましょう。また、富士山の魅力を外国人観光客に説明する英文を考えてみましょう。

_____

_____

◇オーストラリアの巨大岩 Uluru（Ayers Rock）は世界複合遺産に認定されていて、日本人を含め多くの観光客に人気があります。最近その登山が禁止されました。その理由をみんなで調べてみよう。また観光と文化保護の観点で大切なことは何かを考えてみよう。

_____

_____

Reflection

この課で学んだことを評価しよう。

トピックの Can-do		1	2	3	4	5					
文法の Can-do	理解	1	2	3	4	5	活用	1	2	3	4	5
コメント											

世界自然遺産（World Natural Heritage Site）に認定されているのはどの地域？

　　1. 白神山地　　　2. 八丈島　　　3. 種子島

TOPIC **Japanese Cooking**
日本食は「うまみ」が決め手

GRAMMAR 関係詞：関係代名詞

Vocabulary

単語の確認をしよう。(**I know** ☑, **I don't know** ?)

1. ☐ taste (　) 　　2. ☐ element (　) 　　3. ☐ sour (　) 　　4. ☐ bitter (　)
5. ☐ discovery (　) 　6. ☐ glutamate (　) 　7. ☐ inosinic acid (　)
8. ☐ substance (　) 　9. ☐ component (　) 　10. ☐ protein (　)

a. 酸っぱい	b. 物質	c. 要素	d. 苦い	e. 発見
f. グルタミン	g. タンパク質	h. 味	i. イノシン酸	j. 構成要素

|35| ## Listen and fill in the blanks.

1. 私は味噌汁に鰹節を入れます。それで味噌汁がよりおいしくなります。
   I usually put some *katsuobushi* in miso (　　　　), which makes the soup more
   (　　　　).

2. その科学者は偉大な発見をしました。それが人間の味覚に新しい説明を加えました。
   The scientist made a great (　　　　) which gave us a new (　　　　) for
   the human taste system.

3. 泡が表面に浮かんだら鰹節をいれるタイミングです。
   When the (　　　　) come up to the (　　　　), that is the time to put in
   your *katsuobushi.*

4. 日本でよく食べられている豆腐を食べてみてください。
   Please try the (　　　　) curd, tofu, which is often (　　　　) in Japan.

5. 椎茸はかつてブラックマッシュルームと呼ばれていました。
   Shiitake (　　　　) to be called a black (　　　　).

6. 漢字「出汁」は日本人にも読むのが難しいです。
   The Kanji (　　　　) "dashi" are (　　　　) to read even for Japanese
   people.

|36| ## Listen, complete the dialogue and interact.

1. A: What is the Japanese food that you recommend most to your foreign friends?
   B: _____

2. A: Do you know the kind of Japanese sushi which is called *Uramaki?*
   B: _____

3. A: What is the difference between the *Tanuki* in Tokyo and that in Osaka?
   B: _____

4. A: Do you put *wasabi* in the soy sauce dip which is used for sushi?

    B: _____

    So I don't have to put it in the dip.

GRAMMAR 関係詞：関係代名詞

関係代名詞（relative pronoun）は接続詞と代名詞の特徴を併せ持ちます。関係代名詞節（関係代名詞とそれに続く文の形になっています）は前にある名詞（先行詞）を修飾する（説明する）形容詞のような働きをします。また、関係代名詞は文と文をつなぐ役割もしているので、接続詞としての働きもします。

関係代名詞のthatは人やもののどちらでも使えますが、以下のような限定（特定）の意味が強い時にはthatが好まれます。

   This is the house that has the oldest history around here.

[Ⅰ] 以下のa～eの英文が日本語の意味に合うように（　　）内の適切な関係代名詞を選んで文を完成させよう。

a. You can eat *fugu* at the restaurant (who, which) faces the ocean.
あなたはその海に面しているレストランでフグを食べることが出来ます。

b. In Kanto, people eat *unagi* (who, which) is first roasted, then steamed, and roasted again after being dipped in sauce.
関東ではまず焼いて、次に蒸して、タレに浸けてから焼いたウナギを食べます。

c. The chef has two sons, (who, that) are taking over from their father.
コック長には息子が二人居ますが二人とも後を継ごうとしています。

d. Inserting coins and pushing this button here is all (who, that) you have to do.
コインを入れてここにあるボタンを押しさえすればいいです。

e. Don't you know that you have been talking with a chef (who, whose) name is known all over Japan?
あなたは今まで話していたコック長が日本中に名前が知られた人だと言うことを知らないのですか。

[Ⅱ] 次の2つの文を関係代名詞を用いて1つの文にしてみよう。

1. This is a castle. It was built in the Edo period.

   _____.

2. The beautiful temple is a sightseeing spot in this city. *Tokugawa Ieyasu* built it.

   _____.

[Ⅲ] 先行詞の後にコンマを置くことがあります。以下の2つの文に違いがあるか、話し合ってみよう。

a. The mayor has three children who study history.

b. The mayor has three children, who study history.

Before you read

以下の項目を読み、どう思うか数字を書き入れてみよう。

1. ぜひ体験したいと思う　2. 少しそう思う　3. あまりそう思わない　4. 体験したいとは思わない

1. (　) Baking *senbei*.

2. (　) Dining at an old Japanese restaurant.

3. (　) Teaching foreigners how to make *sushi*.

4. (　) Teaching foreigners how to make *miso*.

次にグループを作り、みんなの考えを表にしてみよう。

友人の名前	1問	2問	3問	4問

|37| Read and Think

We have five basic elements of taste. In the past, we only knew about four of these elements: sweet, sour, bitter, and salty. Then, in 1908, the Japanese scientist Ikeda Kikunae found the fifth element. The element of taste that he discovered is called *umami*. When you drink hot water, you taste nothing. When you put *kombu* in the hot water, you taste something. The taste that is added is *umami*.

Japanese cooking that uses *umami* usually takes the taste from two different sources. One of these is *kombu* and the other is *katsuobushi* (dried fish shavings). *Kombu* produces glutamic acid, or glutamate, and *katsuobushi* produces inosinic acid. Both substances come from amino acid, a component of protein. This mixture of two amino acids, which is called *dashi* in Japan, is used in a wide variety of dishes.

(1) Answer the questions.

1. What are the five elements of taste?

_____

2. Who discovered *umami*?

_____

3. What are sources of *umami*?

_____

4. Please write *dashi* in Kanji.

_____

(2) Grammar hunting.

英文から関係代名詞を使っている文を３つ書き出してみよう。次にその中で先行詞を修飾する部分を丸で囲ってみよう。

1. _____
2. _____
3. _____

(3) What do you think?

日本食がブームでいろいろな国でお寿司が食べられます。そのために水産資源が足りなくなる恐れがありますが、あなたはどう思いますか。

Active Plus

◇以下の項目についてあなたはどう思うか数字を書き入れてみよう。

1. おいしいので外国人にぜひ勧めたい	2. 外国人に話題になるから試すように言う
3. 外国人にはあまり勧めない	4. 外国人には食べないように言う

1. (　　) Eating *natto* with only *negi* and soy sauce.
2. (　　) Eating *umeboshi* with cucumber.
3. (　　) Eating *monjayaki* using a spatula.
4. (　　) Eating chicken liver *yakitori*.

◇あなたの友人にそれぞれについてどう思うか尋ねてみよう。

友人の名前	1問	2問	3問	4問

◇あなたの考えと友人の考えを比べて異なる点やその理由などについて意見交換してみよう。

Reflection

この課で学んだことを評価しよう。

トピックの Can-do				1	2	3	4	5					
文法の Can-do	理解	1	2	3	4	5	活用	1	2	3	4	5	
コメント													

1. これは何でしょう？

    a. Sausage   b. Haggis   c. Steak

2. どこで食べることができるでしょうか？

    a. Scotland   b. Germany   c. India

14 Chapter

TOPIC ## Japanized Foreign Culture
日本化した外国文化

GRAMMAR 関係詞：関係副詞

Vocabulary

単語の確認をしよう。(**I know** ☑, **I don't know** ☐)

1. ☐ creativity (　) **2.** ☐ copy (　) **3.** ☐ originality (　) **4.** ☐ turn into (　)
5. ☐ huge (　) **6.** ☐ cosplay (　) **7.** ☐ adapt (　) **8.** ☐ Japanize (　)
9. ☐ show off (　) **10.** ☐ imitate (　)

a. 巨大な	b. 日本化する	c. そっくり写す	d. まねる	e. 変身する
f. 創造性	g. コスプレ	h. 適合させる	i. 独創性	j. 見せびらかす

🎧|38| Listen and fill in the blanks.

1. 日本のマンガやアニメは外国人の若者が日本語を学びたいと思う理由の一つです。
Japanese *manga* and (　　　) are one of the reasons (　　　) young foreign people want to learn the Japanese language.

2. 多くの中国人は有名なアニメの舞台となった鎌倉を訪ねるのが好きです。
Many Chinese people like to visit Kamakura (　　　) scenes of a famous animation (　　　) located.

3. ラーメンは中華料理ではなく、日本人の好みに合わせて「日本化」された中華料理です。
Ramen is not a Chinese (　　　), but a "Japanized" Chinese dish to (　　　) Japanese taste.

4. いつ日本人がクリスマスをお祝いするようになったのか調べてみるのは面白いでしょう。
It would be interesting to (　　　)(　　　) Japanese people started to celebrate Christmas.

5. チキンとケーキは日本人がクリスマスに食べるものです。
Chickens and cakes are (　　　) Japanese people (　　　) on Christmas day.

6. 多くの若者がクリスマスが好きなのはその日に恋人とデートができるからです。
Many young adults like Christmas day (　　　) they can (　　　) their boyfriends and girlfriends.

🎧|39| Listen, complete the dialogue and interact.

1. A: When did Valentine's Day become popular in Japan？？
B: _____

2. A: What is the western Valentine's Day like?
B: _____

3.　A: How different is Japanese Valentine's Day from the western one?

　　B: _____

4.　A: Then, what is White Day? It's very unique to Japan, isn't it?

　　B: _____

5.　A: I've heard that recently the custom of Valentine's Day in Japan is changing.

　　B: _____

GRAMMAR　関係詞：関係副詞

関係副詞（relative adverb）は接続詞と副詞の特徴を併せ持ちます。関係副詞節は先行する場所、時、理由、様態などを修飾（説明）します。また、関係副詞は文と文をつなぐ役割もあるので、接続詞としての働きもします。関係副詞には where, when, why, how があります。

[Ⅰ] 以下のa～dの英文が日本語の意味に合うように（　　）に適当な関係副詞を入れて文を完成させよう。

a.　I like the area of this shrine (　　　) the fall festival is held.
　　私は秋祭りが開催されるこの神社の境内が好きです。

b.　I was born on the day (　　　) the Buddha was born.
　　私は仏陀が誕生した日に生まれました。

c.　This is the reason (　　　) sports festivals are held in many places.
　　これが多くの地域で体育祭が開かれる理由です。

d.　We have to submit a thesis by the time (　　　) we leave school.
　　卒業するまでに論文を提出しなければなりません。

[Ⅱ] 以下の英文a, bの2つの文を関係副詞を用いて1つの文にしてみよう。

a.　*Meiji-jingu* is a shrine. Many people visit the place every year.
　　_____ .

b.　I recommend you come to Japan in summer. You can enjoy fireworks then.
　　_____ .

[Ⅲ] 以下の英文を関係代名詞を使って表現するにはどうすればよいか調べてみよう。

This building is the theater where the New Year's Concert is held.

あなたはハロウィンのお祝いをしますか。また、その時にコスプレをしたことがありますか。お祝いをする / しない理由を簡単に書いてみよう。

Do you celebrate Halloween? (Yes No)

Have you ever "cosplayed" on Halloween? (Yes No)

Reason why you celebrate / don't celebrate : _____

次にグループをつくり、みんなの考えを表にしてみよう。

友人の名前	Celebrate?	Cosplay?	お祝いする / しない理由

Read and Think

　　Many Japanese people celebrate holidays such as Halloween, Christmas, and Valentine's day. Foreign people might think that Japanese people who enjoy these holidays just copy the western tradition. No! Japanese people have turned it into their own unique culture. For example, Japanese Halloween is very different from the Western one. It is a kind of huge "cosplay" parade. Young Japanese adults dress up like popular animation or movie characters. They get together in big towns, such as Shibuya, where large crowds of people enjoy showing off their costumes and taking photos together. This is why the holiday has become very popular in Japan.

　　In the past Japan was said to be good at imitating foreign culture but to lack creativity and originality. However, Japanese people actually add their own ideas to adapt the culture to fit their own country. Now, you can find many "Japanized" elements of foreign culture.

(1) 次の文が本文の内容に合っている場合にはTを、合っていない場合にはFを選んでみよう。

1. Japanese people celebrate Halloween, Christmas, and Valentine's day. （ T F ）
2. Japanese people just copy the western holidays. 　　　　　　　　　　（ T F ）
3. Japanese Halloween is a kind of "cosplay" parade. 　　　　　　　　　（ T F ）
4. People enjoy showing off their costumes and taking photos together. （ T F ）
5. Japanese people think they lack creativity and originality. 　　　　　（ T F ）

(2) Grammar hunting.

英文から関係副詞が使われている文を 2 つ抜き出してみよう。

1. _____

2. _____

(3) What do you think?

「コスプレ」は今海外でも人気になっています。なぜコスプレは人気なのでしょうか？その理由を考えてみよう。

Active Plus

◇日本では、外国の文化（もの）を取り入れるときに表記も日本語風にしてカタカナで表現することがあります。またそれをそのまま言うと英語圏で通じなかったり意味が異なったりすることもあります。そのような例を友人と協力して探してみよう。

例	日本語	英語
1	コンビニ	convenience store
2		
3		
4		
5		

◇ *Tsunami* のように日本語がそのまま英語に取り入れられていることもあります。そのような例を他にも友人と協力して探してみよう。

_____

_____

Reflection

この課で学んだことを評価しよう。

トピックのCan-do			1		2		3		4		5		
文法の Can-do	理解	1	2	3	4	5	活用	1	2	3	4	5	
コメント													

World Quiz

ハロウィンの発祥の地はどこ？

1. Canada　2. England　3. Ireland　4. Sweden

Chapter 15

Project Treasures of Japan
日本の宝物を紹介しよう

Projectのねらい

1. 日本の宝物を紹介する。
2. 学習した英文法を活用して英文を作成する。

モデル英文の分析

1. タイトルを見て全体の内容を予想する。
   写真や挿絵などがあれば、それも活用する。
2. トピックセンテンス（話題文）に書かれていることを読み取る。
3. 紹介する理由としてどのようなことが書かれているか読みとる。
4. 補足的に書かれていることを理解する。
5. まとめの文として書かれていることを理解する。

Enjoy *Onsen*

41

Many Japanese people love *onsen* or hot springs. Japan has many volcanoes, so there are many hot springs with various qualities of water. Each hot spring spa helps you relax and is good for your health.

When you travel around Japan, I recommend you stay in places which have spas. Many Japanese inns and hotels feature *onsen,* so you can easily find good spas. You can also enjoy day spas without spending the night. Bathing in open-air baths will give you a superb experience with nature. Of course, you must not forget to enjoy good local meals.

There are, however, some manners to remember when using a spa. You must bathe naked. When you enter the bath, use the shower or the basins and wash yourself first. Then you can go in and enjoy the spa as you like. Good manners will give you good memories.

英文作成

この活動はできるだけペアやグループで行い、150語程度の英文作成を目標にしよう。

Step 1 ブレーンストーミング
何をテーマに書くか、候補を出し合う。

_____
_____

Step 2 テーマの決定
テーマを決めて紹介する理由を複数 (2, 3程度) 書き出す。

_____
_____

Step 3 補足の洗い出し
追記する事柄の要点を書き出す。

_____
_____

Step 4 執筆開始
タイトルを書いたら大まかな全体の構成を考える。
まず、出だしの文 (トピックセンテンス) 書いて、その後に紹介する理由を書く。
次に補足する事柄を文章にする。
最後にまとめの文を書いて草稿を完成する。

_____
_____
_____
_____
_____

Step 5 相互読み
ペアやグループで草稿を読みあう。分かりやすいか、効果的に書かれているかなどを出し合う。
(評価の観点を参照)

Step 6 修正
内容や展開の見直しを行い、最後に文法や語彙の点検を行う。

Step 7 提出・発表

評価の観点

分かりやすさ	1	2	3	4	5
構成の適切さ	1	2	3	4	5
説得力	1	2	3	4	5
文法・語彙の適切さ	1	2	3	4	5
コメント					

ニッポンの魅力を伝えよう!
基本文法から発信へ

検印
省略

©2021 年 1 月 31 日　第 1 版発行

編著者　大学英語教育学会（JACET）教材研究会
　　　　　　　　　Jenks, Daniel
　　　　　　　　　見上　　　晃
　　　　　　　　　大山　　中勝
　　　　　　　　　鈴木　　彩子
　　　　　　　　　高橋　　貞雄

発行者　　　　　　　　原　　雅　久
発行所　　　　　　株式会社 朝日出版社
　　　　　　〒101-0065 東京都千代田区西神田 3-3-5
　　　　　　　電話　東京　(03) 3239-0271
　　　　　　　FAX　東京　(03) 3239-0479
　　　　　　　E-mail　text-e@asahipress.com
　　　　　　　振替口座　00140-2-46008
　　　　　　　http://www.asahipress.com/
　　　　　　組版／メディアアート　製版／錦明印刷

乱丁・落丁本はお取り替えいたします。
ISBN 978-4-255-15671-2